MILLIONAIRE FOR GOD

Resolis Free Church Sabbath School.

December 1972.

Alistair Matheson.

Ready to risk everything

MILLIONAIRE FOR GOD

The Story of C. T. Studd

by
JOHN T. ERSKINE

LUTTERWORTH PRESS
GUILDFORD AND LONDON

First published 1968
Second Impression 1972
Copyright © 1968 John T. Erskine

FOR DAVID
(My first Grandchild)

ISBN 0 7188 1383 9

PRINTED PHOTOLITHO IN GREAT BRITAIN BY
EBENEZER BAYLIS & SON LIMITED
THE TRINITY PRESS, WORCESTER, AND LONDON

ACKNOWLEDGEMENTS

This shortened version of the thrilling life and work of the famous C. T. Studd has been written with the younger generation in mind, and it is mainly based on Norman Grubb's well-known biography, *C. T. Studd, Cricketer and Pioneer*, first published by Lutterworths in 1933, and still available.

I am grateful, too, to the following: John Pollock for his *The Cambridge Seven* (Inter-Varsity Fellowship), and the China Inland Mission (Overseas Missionary Fellowship) for the loan of two volumes published last century on the work in China.

CONTENTS

1

LIVING ON FOUR PENNIES A DAY

"I DON'T believe even my own mother would know me in this rig-out!"

It was early April, 1885, and the tall, athletic young man was dressed for the first time as a Chinese. He and six like-minded friends, who had sailed with him to China, arriving there not many months before, were about to split up. They were to make their varying ways far inland, even to the remotest parts of the country where white men had never been seen.

They felt they had been chosen by God to tell the heathen people of China all about the Lord Jesus Christ and His salvation.

This group of young men, who had been at Cambridge University together, had been given the title of The Cambridge Seven long before they had left England. They had been together for some months in Shanghai, and had decided that before they went to trek, they must dress like the Chinese —in skirts and long-sleeved gowns, with cowl-like hats, and, of course, pigtails; and they must live rough and eat exactly the same food, cooked the same way as the poverty-stricken nationals of that vast land.

They were convinced that the only way to get their story over to the Chinese was to *be* Chinese.

Charles Thomas Studd—C.T. for short—was the one who felt most unlike a Chinese. As he was very tall, he would be very conspicuous among the short nationals.

He felt he was at another disadvantage. He had huge feet, too, and the Chinese prided themselves on their small ones.

But C.T. was not the kind of fellow to go about groaning over such points as these. He was sure that God would take care of any such difficulties that arose.

All the same, his feet *were* a problem; he found he couldn't get a pair of shoes large enough for them. The first shoemaker who called on him said he had never made a pair of shoes *that* size, and he refused point-blank to attempt such a "gigantic operation". In fact, he fled from the house before the evil spirits could get hold of him.

Another craftsman was found who would make a pair to the required size. He said, however, that it would be a pioneering effort on his part, and that he couldn't be sure of the results. He had never seen any feet like C.T.'s before.

Charles Studd began his travels with two other members of The Seven who were brothers. He went with them 1,800 miles up the Yangtse and Han rivers to Hanchung. The journey took them three months, and from there, C.T. struck north to Pingyang-fu, with two Christian colporteurs (itinerant sellers of books, booklets and tracts).

What an adventure that was for C.T.! Sleeping in dirty inns, ploughing through mud, sometimes up to the knees in it, and at other times struggling across stony and rocky ground.

His feet were his major trouble. They became very sore, and one day he decided he must take off his stronger footwear and put on sandals—of a sort. Made of straw and string, at every step they cut deeper into the flesh, so the thirty miles covered that day were a long-term agony.

Worse was to come. Next day he knew he couldn't stand the sandals any longer, so he had to trudge many many weary miles barefoot. The result was seven raw places, most of them on one foot.

The next day was a thirty-eight-mile stretch, each step of which was "like a knife going into my feet". Most of that day he had to face up to things alone, because he couldn't manage his companions' rate of progress.

The badly-affected foot became very puffy and

extremely sore, but somehow C.T. did get to journey's end.

Came the day when the situation was so serious that he asked one of the colporteurs whether he would agree to anoint him with oil as described in the Epistle of James, chapter 5, verses 14 and 15.

The colporteur was a bit doubtful at first about doing this, because he hadn't been asked to do anything like it before. But, at length, he agreed. "I believed the Lord would heal my foot if this were done," C.T. wrote later. "And my foot did get better rapidly after the anointing."

A man of great faith, the next day C.T. believed the foot was getting better—though it didn't *look* a bit like it—and he walked quite a long way on it. That night, it wasn't so swollen, and he continued to manage twenty miles a day. The swelling and the soreness had disappeared, and the foot which had been the worse by far was now as good as the other one.

That was an early personal experience of faith healing for C.T., and he thanked God for it.

On another occasion, while on a houseboat, he and his companions got rid of a host of rats which stole their socks while they were asleep, and nibbled off their legging tapes to make their "homes" comfortable. How did C.T. and his friends do it? Not by setting traps, but by asking

God to rid them of this menace to their missionary work.

C.T. was in Pingyang by November, and there he enjoyed long days full of action. He used to wake about 3.30 a.m., and have a "good read" in the Bible, which exercise he once called "a large dose of spiritual champagne".

He said that he found what he read so early in the morning was stamped indelibly on his mind all through the day. If he missed this time, he felt like Samson shorn of his hair, and so of all his strength.

In the late spring of 1886, C.T. spent some months completely alone among the Chinese at Chin-Wu. Much of the hottest part of the days was spent in Bible reading, prayer and meditation, but an hour or so before sunset each day, he would go out with his tracts, Gospel portions, and, of course, his beloved Chinese New Testament, given to him before he left Britain.

How he loved the talks he had with the locals about his one and only hero, Jesus Christ, whose Gospel he sought to proclaim at every possible moment. And how glad he was to be able to talk to them in their own language!

At Chin-Wu, C.T. had a cook whom he named Friday. C.T. had to restrain the man for he thought his "boss" should live—at any rate so far as food was concerned—like a rich mandarin. Actually, C.T.'s food cost him about four pennies per day; it was mostly rice.

C.T. went to Hanchung with Hudson Taylor, the leader of the China Inland Mission, of which all The Cambridge Seven were members.

It may have been on this trek that the missionaries had many miraculous escapes getting across narrow mountain ledges while rocks kept falling around them; fording streams the jet-speed of the current of which carried them off their feet.

In the narrow gorges or defiles, the walls were almost perpendicular and over 100 ft. high. In the rainy season there were landslips which, if small, made quagmires. Two of the mules got involved in one of these, and floated in the mire on their sides. C.T. had to wade into the mud and help raise the packs off the animals' backs, and get the packs carried away singly by the muleteers. Then the animals, struggling hard, did manage to get out of the bog. But what a time it took; and how near the danger line they often were!

Arrived at Hanchung, the trekkers heard of the riots in Szchuan, and that the foreigners had had to flee for their lives from Chungking, the local capital.

Hudson Taylor at once asked his men, "Any volunteers for Szchuan?" Everyone who could be spared volunteered, and C.T. was chosen to go with a friend named Phelps. Their orders were very simple. They were to "retake the place". Just those three words, no ifs or buts.

It took the two men an exciting three days to get to Pauling. The innkeepers there wouldn't accept any non-Chinese; they were in great fear of being accused of harbouring "foreign devils". The two men found, however, a room of sorts without a window. One side of the place was next to a pigsty, there being only thin boards between.

The next night they did manage to get into an inn in another part of the town.

"Well, at the worst, this room *does* have a window!" commented C.T., but they found the smells there were worse than anything they had experienced up to then.

Smells were not the main trouble, however. In the middle of the first night, C.T., sleepless and irritating all over, had to get up and start a pitched battle with hundreds of bed-bugs.

"I bagged twenty-five brace to my own gun," he wrote later, using the language of the moneyed, sport-loving home in which he had been brought up, "without beaters or dogs. Not bad for an hour's sport!"

When at length Studd and Phelps reached the centre of Chungking, the British Consul there couldn't believe his eyes when two fellow-countrymen came into his room.

"However did you manage to get here?" he asked. "There are guards at every one of the city's gates to prevent any 'foreign devils' from getting in."

The missionaries just smiled, and told him that God had made a way for them to get inside the city, and then added the reason for their coming—to recapture Szchuan for the Lord.

The Consul's face showed his amazement.

"Well, whatever else you do, you can't stay here anyway!" was the answer. "I can give you a passport to go either up or down the river, but I'm the only foreigner allowed to live in this city."

Finally the Consul suggested they should stay to dinner, and in the middle of the meal, he suddenly, and most surprisingly, said, "Studd, will you stay with me?"

The Consul didn't attempt to explain his change of front, and C.T. wrote home of the incident, "I didn't know till some time afterwards why God had sent me to that place."

2

TAKEN FOR A RIDE

"HERE IS a letter from father asking us to meet him in London on Saturday," said C. T. Studd to his brothers, Kynaston and George, who were with him at school at Eton in 1877.

"Does he say what he wants us for?" asked Kynaston, better known by his initials J.E.K., or as Kinny.

"No he doesn't; but he says it's something special," was C.T.'s reply.

"I expect he'll take us to a theatre, or to see the Christy Minstrels" (one of the best-known groups of those days).

"We'll have to wait and see, won't we?" remarked C.T., and they made their plans for the journey to London on the Saturday.

When they met Edward Studd, all the boys seemed dimly aware of a difference in him, but they did not remark on it to him. They hadn't heard that a great change had recently come over his whole way of life.

"Where are you taking us, sir?" asked C.T., for

he was the most eager to have the puzzle solved.

"Oh, didn't I tell you, my boy?" was Edward Studd's smiling reply, which made the lads the more eager to know. "Well, I'd better do so now, hadn't I? We're going to a theatre—the famous one in Drury Lane, to see and hear someone very special. I'm sure you'll like him."

Kinny asked for more details, but his father was silent as they set off for Drury Lane. The boys had a real shock when, nearing the theatre, they saw some placards announcing that two famous American evangelists, Dwight L. Moody and Ira D. Sankey, were holding meetings there.

"Oh, glory be, it's a pi-show!" whispered C.T. to George, the expression on whose face showed exactly what he thought of it.

The young Studds had been brought up to obey their parents without question, so in they went. The theatre was well-filled, and the people in the audience were singing hymns of a kind they had never heard before. One of them was something about a roll being called up yonder.

Soon Moody and Sankey appeared on the platform, and the meeting got under way.

The earlier part of the programme left the three boys cold, but C.T. most certainly pricked up his ears very soon after Moody began to speak. He listened attentively, but fidgeted. It couldn't be said that he was really interested and certainly in no way moved or thrilled. He just didn't feel it had anything to do with him personally.

But C.T. *did* notice that the kind of religion about which Moody was talking with such fervour was much more dynamic and attractive than the "Sunday best, and forget all about it on Monday" stuff he and his brothers had been used to. There was a purpose in the kind of Christianity Moody claimed was the only one that mattered.

After the meeting, Edward Studd must have taken his sons somewhere to talk things over, for after this London visit the lads learned that their father had been taken to hear Moody by a friend; had been to hear the evangelist a second time; and that Moody had "had it out" with him so successfully that Edward Studd accepted the Lord Jesus as his personal Saviour and committed his life to him. He became a completely different man. In fact, his coachman said of him, "Though the master has the same skin, there's a new man inside it."

Edward Studd was quick to give up all his horse-racing, his card-playing, his dancing, and his many other social activities, and to concentrate on bringing all his family and friends to accept this new life of service for Christ which he found so much more worth while than his old interests.

But the three brothers—and especially C.T.—
took a dim view of their father's evangelistic zeal.
C.T. said that "everyone in their home had a dog's
life until they were converted".

C.T. himself tried all sorts of ruses to escape
having quiet talks with his parent; but it wasn't
his father in the end who got through to him first.
It was a man named Weatherby, and C.T. didn't
come in contact with him until the holidays a year
later.

Edward Studd had turned one of the halls in
their family home at Tedworth, in Wilts, into a
place where Sunday Christian meetings could be
held. There were two speakers each weekend, and
this time one was popular with the boys and the
other was not.

"I can't stand old Weatherby," said C.T. to his
brothers on the Saturday morning. "Let's have a
bit of fun with him. He says he can ride a bit, but
that he's not much of a horseman. Let's get him to
come out with us——"

"And we'll be on the racers father gave us
recently?" put in one of the brothers.

"Smashing idea!" they chorused. "We'll ride
slowly behind at first, and then pass old Weatherby
and father at the canter. The two horses will go
all out to get level with us, and we shall see what
we shall see!"

What they saw was that Weatherby had a great deal more guts than they expected. He managed, though not without considerable difficulty, to keep his seat, and the boys' opinion of him changed.

That afternoon, the visitor stopped C.T. on his way to the paddock cricket-ground.

"Spare me a few minutes, Charles?" he asked, and C.T. felt he had to do so, because of the trick they had played on him earlier.

The visitor's first question as they sat on a near-by tree was, "Are you a Christian, Charles?"

C.T. didn't reply for a moment, then he said, "I don't suppose I'm what *you'd* call a Christian, but I've believed in Jesus ever since I was knee high—and in the Church, too."

C.T. hoped the answer would satisfy his questioner because he was eager to get to the wicket. But it didn't. There followed a long question-and-answer period based on the Nicodemus story in John 3, stressing that it was because God loved the world so much that He gave His Son so that those who believed in Him should not perish but have everlasting life—a wonderful gift.

"You *do* usually say thank you to a person for a gift, don't you, Charles?" Weatherby put to him. "Well, don't you think *that* gift is very much worth saying thank you for? Will you do just that? You'll never regret it!"

At that moment a bell rang for C.T. He said some time afterwards that, as he did say thank you, a wonderful sense of peace and joy came to him, and a knowledge of the meaning of what Jesus described to Nicodemus as a must—being "born again", and so having the gift of eternal life.

That same day, Weatherby tackled both the other lads and won them over. None of them told anyone about it, but when they returned to Eton, they each wrote separately to their father, and had a joint letter back from him saying how very glad he was that they had all made the great decision.

The three Studds had made up their minds that they must let others know of their decisions, and they started a Bible Class at Eton. But so far as C.T. was concerned, his first love was still cricket. The three young fellows played together in the first eleven only once—and there were many remarks by the opposition about being "all right when they'd collared the Three Studds".

C.T. captained the eleven in 1879, and proved himself a great all-rounder. He joined his two brothers at Trinity College, Cambridge, in that same year, won his Blue and played for the university for four consecutive years, captaining the side for one season.

The year 1882 saw C.T. at the height of his form. He was chosen what would be called now Cricketer of the Year, having scored two centuries against the Australians. He was in the England team which was beaten by the Aussies at the Oval —their first win against England—and after which the famous term "The Ashes" broke into the language of cricket, through an epitaph in a sporting paper.

The famous batsman W. G. Grace said C.T. was "the most brilliant member of a well-known cricketing family . . . his batting and bowling were very good."

C.T.'s career at Cambridge has been described as "one long blaze of cricketing glory". He himself said he made a serious business of the game. He never regretted his passion for cricket, but he *did* regret that he had made an idol of the game. He agreed, however, that he did learn lessons of courage, self-denial, self-control and endurance, which were later much used in his work as a missionary.

C.T. confessed that his Christian life was very low down in the list of his priorities at that time. He called it "an unhappy, backslidden state". In later life, he never could forget this black period, and did his utmost to point out the dangers arising from loss of faith.

In his early days in China, he wrote to his younger brothers, then at Eton, "I don't say, don't play games, or cricket and so forth. By all means play and enjoy them, giving thanks to Jesus for them. Only take care that games don't become an idol to you as they did to me.

"What good will it do to anybody in the next world to have been the best player that ever has been?" he pointed out to them. "And, then, think of the difference between that and winning people for Jesus!"

C.T. became very mixed-up and, following the shock of watching his devout brother George hovering between life and death, he felt he must go and hear Moody (who was again in Britain) once more. He got his faith back at that meeting.

"Better than all else," he said of that event, "God set me to work for Him—trying to persuade my friends to read the Gospel story and let it influence their lives.

"But I became restless and anxious," he went on. "My health gave way and I had to go into the country to recuperate. I came back much better, but I still didn't know exactly what God wanted me to do."

The one thing clear to him was that he must have the power of which Christ spoke, and he found the way to get it through reading a book

entitled *The Christian's Secret of a Happy Life*.
Priority No. 1 for him must be a childlike faith,
coupled with the decision to trust God in *everything*.

To his own amazement, he felt strongly drawn
to take up missionary work in a foreign land, and
he was sure that China was to be the country
chosen by God for his pioneering efforts. But his
own family—and especially his beloved mother—
were dead against the idea. In fact, a relation
told him that the plan was breaking his mother's
heart.

"But I knew God had given me my marching
orders to go to China," wrote C.T. of this period
of conflict, and he refused to budge from his
position. Before he left for China, he had the joy
of knowing that his mother had come round to his
way of thinking, and he was fully conscious of her
prayers for him when he was "up against it" in
that heathen land.

A number of his friends were deeply interested
in the work of the China Inland Mission, and on
Tuesday, November 4, 1884, he went to the H.Q.
of the Mission at Mildmay, in North London,
talked to Director Hudson Taylor about his call to
China, and was accepted as an associate member of
the Mission.

C.T.'s friend Stan Smith also applied, and very

soon five other fellows joined them—and The Cambridge Seven came into being.

Came the time when Studd and Smith went back to Cambridge, with Hudson Taylor, and held a Mission there. The "spiritual millionaires", as someone called them, were a big success, and from then on, the missionaries were almost over-whelmed with calls on their services in crusades all over Great Britain.

The first time The Cambridge Seven were all together on a platform was at the Exeter Hall, in London, on January 8, 1885. C.T.'s message was straight from the shoulder, witnessing to the wonderful value of having a personal Saviour. It was in the same hall that the final of many Farewell Meetings was held almost a month later.

"I want to recommend you tonight to my Master," were C.T.'s opening words. "I have tried many ways of pleasure in my time; I have been run-ning after the best master—and thank God I have found Him . . . What are you really living for? . . . Better take His word, and implicitly obey it . . . There is enough power in this meeting," he told his audience later, prophetically, "to stir not only London and England, but the whole world!"

At nine-thirty the next morning (February 5), The Cambridge Seven—Monty Beauchamp, Bill Cassels, Teddy Hoste, Arthur and Cecil Polhill-

Turner, Stan Smith, and Charlie Studd—set off from Victoria Station to Dover on their long journey to Shanghai, which they reached on March 18.

3

"GOD CAN'T CHANGE *ME*!"

"I WON'T sign it!" It was the British Consul at Chungking speaking to C. T. Studd, and it sounded as definite a refusal as on the previous occasion.

What C.T. had asked him to do was to sign papers the missionary had drawn up to give someone a power of attorney—that is, the right for him to act over money matters. The papers needed the signature of one of Queen Victoria's officers in China.

C.T. needed the papers for an amazing reason. It was because he had decided to give away all the money his father, who had died two years after his conversion, had left to him. The provisional figure was well over £25,000: a lot of money today, but a huge fortune in those times.

His reading of certain New Testament passages had brought C.T. to this decision—especially the reply by Jesus to the rich young ruler who asked how to get eternal life: "Sell that thou hast, and give to the poor . . . take up thy cross and follow

Me." In C.T.'s view that was for *his* day just as much as for Christ's own time.

When Charlie called on the Chungking Consul he knew he was now in a position to distribute the money, and on his list was a gift of £5,000 to Moody to start Gospel work in Tirhoot, in North India, where C.T.'s father had made his huge fortune. Moody found he could not do this then; instead he started the Moody Bible Institute in Chicago, now world-famous for its training of missionaries and its wonderful colour films.

The Consul could not see the sense of the missionary's decision, so he said to him, "Look here, you take two weeks to think it over, and if you haven't changed your mind—and I hope you *will* have—I'll sign the documents for you."

On their first meeting, it was the Consul who suddenly changed his mind and invited C.T. to stay with him. This time he had to take back his refusal, for Charlie was determined to go ahead with his plan for getting rid of his worldly wealth.

The final total of his legacy was much greater than £25,000, so he donated many more thousands to good causes, but he did keep back about £3,000, not to spend but just in case there should be any difficulties over the distribution of the money.

Later C.T. offered this balance to his fiancée,

Priscilla Stewart, just before their wedding. But she flatly refused to accept it.

"Charlie," she said, "what exactly did the Lord tell the rich young man to do?"

"Sell everything he had," was the quick reply.

"Well, then, we'll start in the clear with the Lord at our wedding." And they sent the money to General Booth of the Salvation Army, the gift to be acknowledged as from "Go, and do thou likewise."

This action was characteristic of Scilla Stewart. She was as earnest and self-forgetting a Christian as her husband. Born in Lisburn, near Belfast, she had blue eyes and golden hair; she was a high-spirited girl out for a good time. After her conversion, which came about through a dream, she attended Salvation Army meetings.

"I walked in their processions," she used to say in telling of those early days. "And how worth while it was! Old boots were thrown at us, and wood, stones, rotten eggs, and oranges. None of my friends recognized me in the street, and all the young men who were fond of me walked on the other side."

Charlie Studd arrived back in Shanghai from his station in North China about the same time that Scilla landed at the port to start her missionary career. She had considerable difficulty over the climate, but one of her active interests was in a Rest Home for Servicemen. It was there that she met C.T., and the attraction was mutual.

In course of time, Scilla was detailed to travel up the Yangtse to Ta-Ku-Tang, while C.T.'s orders were to return to Taiyuen-Fu, in the far north.

The two young people entered into a prolonged correspondence; some of C.T.'s letters were of nearly seventy pages! When she turned down his proposal, he replied in his characteristic forthright way, "I intend to marry you whether you will or not, so you had better make up your mind and accept the situation."

And she did.

They had an unofficial wedding first, taken by a Chinese evangelist at Scilla's mission station. They were, in their own words, "united to fight for Jesus", and they promised never to hinder each other from serving Him. The official wedding was by a British Consul at Tientsin.

When they left Tientsin on their wedding day, they had in the world only five dollars and some bedding. They travelled to Lungang-Fu with Miss Burroughes to start a pioneer work in that inland city. The going was terribly hard. They were "foreign devils" and everything that went wrong in the area, including a long drought, was blamed on them.

They spent seven years in Lungang-Fu, and for most of the time they did not go outside the door without being shouted at and cursed.

A "wicked old man", as Scilla described him, let them rent a house he owned, only because it was haunted and so no Chinese would live in it. Scilla did not say how many rooms it had, but all the walls were whitewashed and the floors were of brick. There was a fireplace in the centre, and a brick bed, the bricks of which were neither even nor level, and the "mattress" was a thin cotton-wool quilt.

That was the Studds' bed for three years of their time at Lungang-Fu. Then it became a homing-place for scorpions, so the Studds had to demolish it and use planking. Very likely the house had many other undesirable residents, such as very wild stray cats, rats, bats, and mosquitoes. The Studds probably used newspapers to decorate the walls, as other missionaries did at that time.

By opening every corner of their house to the locals, thus taking full advantage of the Chinese love for prying into other people's lives, the missionaries managed gradually to get on fairly familiar terms with a proportion of the inhabitants. Gradually, too, they saw a few men and women change from idol-worshippers to believers in

Christ. These made light of the vilest persecution. Here is the story of one of them:

"I'm a murderer, an adulterer. I've broken all the laws again and again. I'm also a confirmed opium smoker. Your God can't do anything to change *me*!"

So said a man who remained behind alone after a meeting, but C.T. talked to him about the love of Jesus and the power of the Holy Spirit, and the man was converted. The first thing he said was almost unbelievable and very wonderful.

"I must go at once to the town where I did all these evil things, and tell them all you've told me!" he exclaimed.

And he did.

Crowds came to hear him, and this enraged the heathen leaders, who had him up before the local mandarin. His punishment was 2,000 strokes with a bamboo cane, and he was in a terrible state when it was over. In fact he was left for dead, but he was rescued by kindly folk and taken to hospital, only to return as soon as he could to the place where he had been beaten.

They put him in prison this time, instead of beating him. But the prison had small open windows, and slits in the walls, so he shouted his Gospel message through them. Crowds came to hear him again, and the mandarin decided he would do less harm if he were free.

"We can't hope to move anyone as stubborn as he is," he said.

Drug addicts were among the most difficult people whom C.T. tried to help. He spent a great deal of time in the Opium Refuge, dealing, after the first two men had been cured of their horrible habit, with as many as fifty addicts at once. Some of the cures took only a month.

*   *   *

Lungang-Fu was far from any white doctor. When the Studds' first child was on the way, Scilla was seriously ill, but to travel, if she could do it, to see a doctor would mean months away from their station.

"I don't see how it can possibly be managed," said C.T. "So why not rely completely on Dr. Jesus? I'm sure there's no need to assure you, darling, that He'll manage things perfectly."

Scilla was anointed with oil as her husband had been at the time of his foot trouble, and Grace arrived safely. Three more children, all girls, were born to the Studds in Lungang-Fu: Praise (Dorothy), Prayer (Edith), and Joy (Pauline). A fourth lived only one day.

The Studds lived then, as they had always done,

by faith, though they had a small allowance from their Society. Although they dressed and ate as the Chinese did, they were often almost penniless and near to starvation. But C.T. and Scilla experienced not only God's power to heal, but also the miracle of His provision for them, when the present and the future looked very black.

On one occasion when the postman's fortnightly call had not brought any letters with financial help for their work, C.T. said, "We must look facts in the face, Scilla. If the postman doesn't bring us some help in two weeks' time, we shall be right up against it. Let's tell God about it—though He knows, of course, already."

They stayed on their knees for twenty minutes, and rose with a new sense of His presence and power. The postman returned at his appointed time, and they were quick to open the bag.

The handwriting on one letter was unknown to them. C.T. tore open the envelope, and out dropped a piece of paper. Neither stooped to pick it up as Charles read, "I have for some reason or other received the command of God to send you a cheque for £100. I have never met you. I have only heard of you, and that not often . . . Why God should command me to send you this, *I* don't know. *You'll* know better than I. Anyhow, here it is, and I hope it will do you good."

Do them good! It did much more than that!

Scilla was a little dizzy as she bent to pick up the paper-miracle, which she handed to C.T. with a radiant smile.

"Isn't God marvellous!" she breathed. "It will certainly do us good, won't it?" She looked up to the makeshift roof and added, "Oh, thank You, thank You, Father dear!"

The name on the cheque was Frank Crossley, and when C.T. went home on furlough, he met Crossley, and they became close friends and fellow-workers in evangelism.

The Studds went home in 1894 when a war between Japan and China was raging. They had a wonderful send-off from the mission station, but the journey to the coast was pretty tough with the four children. They did not dare to take women to look after the children, because they would have been accused of stealing them; but the two male nurses were very useful.

Part of the journey was by sedan chairs carried by two mules—the chair in the middle and a mule at each end, with two long poles acting as "shafts". A cargo-boat trip followed, and then they transferred to a house-boat.

Things looked grim when they were near Tienstin, for whenever they wanted to land, a huge crowd gathered. This is where their daughter

Grace came to the rescue. She could speak the language and so she was able to answer all their questions about the "foreign devils". "What is your age and name? What sort of food do you eat? Have you any? Where are you going? And why?"

The people were amazed that she was able to answer them in their own tongue, and as Grace went on replying, an ugly crowd became a friendly one. "You see, this child talks our language because she eats our food," they said.

But language *was* a problem for Grace and her three sisters when they reached their grandmother's home in London, for none of them could speak a word of English!

4

"WHAT'S SO TASTY ABOUT CHRISTIANS?"

"YOU shouldn't make them ride on such a high-spirited pony as Gamecock!" protested Scilla Studd, after the fourth of their daughters had been flung over the pony's head.

But C.T. took no notice of what his wife said.

"You mustn't let the idea of fear get into their heads," he countered, "or they'll become cowards. They must learn to ride Gamecock, for if they master that pony, they'll not be afraid to ride anything."

The four girls were having one of their earliest riding lessons with their father, who had had plenty of experience with horses in his younger days. The girls had recently come out with their mother to Ootacamund, in South India, where their father was now in charge of the Union Church, an independent place of worship, run by the Anglo-Indian Evangelization Society.

C.T. had come to India almost at the end of the nineteenth century to work in the Tirhoot area (where his father had made a fortune as a tea-planter) and had stayed there for six months, in which many folk of all ranks had accepted Christ as their Saviour.

C.T. was in Ootacamund for six thrill-packed years, though for much of the time he was a martyr to asthma, being unable to sleep except between the hours of two and four in the morning. "Charlie is a wreck," Scilla wrote home, "and almost the slightest movement brings on asthma." But he stuck it out, and so did Scilla, and he lived to spend eighteen years in the heart of then Darkest Africa.

How C.T. loved to have his children, known in the family as The Clan, with him! How keen he was to teach them to be courageous and fearless, not only through horse-riding, but by facing up to whatever problems came their way; keen to teach them to believe in themselves, but above all to get them to see, while still so young, that the only really worthwhile life was one given back to God for Him to use as He felt best.

So it is not surprising to be able to record that all four girls decided for Christ during the pastorate at Ootacamund, and that all four were baptized at the same time.

The fact that The Clan would not be split up even for such a ceremony led to a most unusual, if not unique, baptismal service. Because Union was an independent church, which did not have a baptistry, C.T. had to perform the ceremony himself, and he had to find a way round the difficulty.

He decided to make his own plans, at home.

"I ordered the gardener to dig up one of the biggest flower-beds to a substantial depth," he described later, "then I went down to one of the commercial houses in the town and purchased the biggest zinc-lined packing case I could find. When it was delivered, we fitted it into the flower-bed hole."

Another hole beside it was dug for the pastor to stand in, but that hole was not to have any water in it.

The morning planned for the baptismal service was very cold, and so a procession of native boys carried relays of kettles and saucepans of all shapes and sizes full of hot water to the "baptistry". They had great difficulty in keeping up the level of the water, because the "tank" sprang a small leak.

After answering questions about what they believed, one by one the girls stepped into the water, and were dipped under, while appropriate singing was going on.

Though they all knew it was a most solemn occasion, C.T. recalled that "I'm afraid my girls

... imbibed the spirit of fun which possessed us. At any rate, after the ceremony the girls got it off on me that I had baptized two of them with the wrong names."

★   ★   ★

The family returned to England in 1906, and C.T. went back into evangelism, his meetings having a special slant for men. The calls on his services were almost overwhelming, for his bluntness, his sense of humour, his direct speaking in a language men would understand and with illustrations from masculine activities, caught and held their attention.

Listen to the sort of thing he said at a businessmen's luncheon:

"Gentlemen," he would say, "you've had a rich dinner; you'll be ready for plain-speaking . . . I shall speak in ordinary—not pulpit or academic—language that we're all accustomed to use when engaged in the real battle of life, or in heart-to-heart talking.

"I once had another religion—mincing, lisping, bated-breath, proper, hunting the Bible for hidden truths; but no obedience, no sacrifice. Then came the change . . . Soft speech became crude salt . . . Words became deeds. The commands of Christ became not merely Sunday recitations, but battle calls to be obeyed, unless one would lose one's self-respect and manhood.

"Instead of saying 'Lord, Lord' in a most reverent voice many times and yet continuing deaf to the simplest commandments, I began to look upon God as really my Father . . . and to trust Him as such. Instead of talking about fellowship, I enjoyed it. Instead of being unnatural, I became natural—and unconventional.

"I talked of God and Jesus Christ as real living personal friends and relations—and *they* have never chided me for it! . . . In other words, I dropped cant and ceremony and became a Christian."

In the coming years, God showed more vividly than He had ever done before in the life of C. T. Studd what He can do with a son or daughter of His who is surrendered to Him for service, without any questions or doubts.

This period of his life lasted until he was on a visit to Liverpool in 1908, and saw a notice outside a building with these words: CANNIBALS WANT CHRISTIANS.

That phrase touched his keen sense of humour, and he asked himself, as he stood staring at the board, "I wonder what's so specially tasty about Christians for a meal?" He laughed aloud. "I'll go inside and find out what sort of person could have put up such a notice."

The "culprit" was, he presumed correctly, the foreigner who was speaking when he entered and sat down—speaking in thrilling words of his experiences, of his life-and-death struggles, while on trek in the heart of then Darkest Africa. He said that there were many many tribes there living in complete heathen darkness, having never heard the story of Jesus and His love.

"Explorers, big-game hunters have been there," said Dr. Karl Kumm, "and have never even thought of the natives' need! Arabs, traders of other sorts, European officials, and scientists have endured all sorts of hardships to open up the country from a commercial point of view, but no Christian—not a single one!—has ever been in the places I'm thinking of, let alone tried to live there so as to get to know the natives and tell them about God's Son who was—and is—as much their Saviour as yours and mine! Why doesn't someone go? Why doesn't somebody hear and answer God's call? . . . Why don't *you* go?"

C.T. thought the speaker pointed directly at him, and much of what Dr. Kumm said later rolled like waves over the listener's head. He sat there uncomfortably questioning himself, seeking to relieve the deep sense of shame which he felt.

"Why haven't any Christians gone?" he asked himself. "Why haven't *you* gone?" "Well, I haven't gone," he answered, "because no one has ever made me realize the urgent, the desperate need of the Africans. And I haven't gone because I'm positive the doctors wouldn't let me. So what's the use . . .?"

Then he felt that God spoke directly to him. "Why don't *you* go? You know I am the Good Physician, and so I can see you through all the way to the heart of Africa, and I can keep you there. Remember what My Son said—that I could supply *all* you need?"

That put the seal on C.T.'s already almost-made decision. There could be no more excuses; there shouldn't ever have been any. He had received God's call to go to Africa, and that he would do, with God's help, overcoming all obstacles.

This was, he felt, the greatest project of his life; this was the reason why he had had all those experiences in evangelism in Britain and all that missionary work in China and in India. They had been training for this day, and the days to come.

But of course he must be practical. How was he to set about it? The first thing to do was to make himself known to Dr. Kumm, and tell him of his decision, adding that he was fifty now, and had had fifteen years of ill-health. How long could he hope to survive in tropical Africa?

They had many talks, and their first definite plan was to cross Africa together, starting from the Niger side. "This was the only time that God agreed with the doctors," C.T. said of this period. "I was ready to go against doctors' orders, but the Lord put me to bed with malaria, and plainly said 'No!'"

The next plan was a journey to Southern Sudan, a thousand miles south of Khartoum. A group of business men said they would support him financially provided he was passed by the doctor. The M.O.'s report was a very definite "No!"

The business men's committee required a promise that he would not venture south of Khartoum. This C.T. refused to give, so they refused to help him financially.

Everything, and everybody, seemed against him, yet he was still certain that God wanted him in Africa. He sat pondering what to do, and his thoughts went back over the past.

In his student days, he had given up a promising career and gone to China. In that vast land he had lived as a native, had given away all his wealth, and had relied entirely on God. In India, he had been plagued by ill-health, but God had seen him through, and he had had the joy of baptizing all his four children. Surely he could justly claim that he

was in line with the great "gamblers of faith"—
Abraham, Isaac, Peter, Paul, and all those who
had followed them.

He knew now what he would do. He would stick
to his decision, and tell the committee that not
even their refusal to support him financially could
stop him from penetrating into the heart of Africa
to tell the people there about Jesus.

"I will blaze the trail," he wrote to them,
"though my grave may only become a stepping
stone that younger men may follow."

Three weeks before C.T. was due to sail (and
Dr. Kumm seems to have dropped out of the story
hereabouts) he had no money for his passage. He
was booked to speak in Birmingham and then in
Liverpool to audiences who did not know the
problem he had on his mind. In both places he
spoke with great power and inspiration, not
mentioning his financial needs.

When he was saying goodbye to the people who
had planned the Liverpool meetings, a man he
had never seen before put £10 into his hand. How
his eyes lit up with excitement! This is what he
had hoped for. It was a sign that he was now to
make practical plans.

"I'll go straight to the shipping company's
office here in Liverpool," he said to himself, "and
book my passage to Port Said. And I'll tell the

committee what I've done, that I will!" And he smiled broadly.

That act of faith was well rewarded, for help came to him in many wonderful and unexpected ways, though, as with his decision for China, it was his nearest and dearest relation who didn't approve. Scilla felt that the whole plan was far too much for him, and that it wasn't what God wanted him to do.

He set sail on December 15, 1910, however, and he always claimed that, in his cabin on the first night at sea, God spoke to him in words which indeed proved to be prophetic.

"This trip is not merely for the Sudan," C.T. felt God say to him, "it is for the whole unevangelized world."

Such an idea seemed utterly impossible—but faith doesn't have such a word in its dictionary.

"Every place your foot shall tread upon," C.T. felt He also said, "I have given it to you."

Telling a friend about this, he wrote: "Thank God I have big feet!"

He wrote a lot of letters while on board, many of them to Scilla, and they must have helped her eventually to see that it *was* God's call.

He wrote, too, about a great idea which had come to him. He called it A New Crusade. She was in poor health at the time and he assured her that her health would be restored; that she would become a bigger firebrand for Jesus than she had ever been, and that their daughters would be "white-hot Christian warriors". "And God grant that, as a silver wedding present, He will give us this noble work to do for Him in Africa. You and I will do it, and others shall rise up and follow."

Reaching Khartoum, C.T. became caught up in both religious and social activities. He held the first mission in that town, and was invited to dine at Sir Reginald Wingate's palace several times, though he did not get on very well with dress shirts!

Of course C.T. was often reminded by people there of his cricketing successes, and at one dinner a lady sitting next to him told him that she had been present at the Cambridge University *v.* The Australians match in 1882.

"You made the winning hit to the boundary where I was sitting," the lady said, "and the ball rolled under my petticoat. I stooped down, picked it up, and threw it back. I have regretted doing so ever since. I ought to have kept it, had a silver band put round it and presented it to you."

There were heavy casualties on the first trek he made with the Bishop of Khartoum and Archdeacon Shaw, but the deaths were not human; they were donkeys. The men started out with twenty-nine donkeys on their exploration of the Bahr-el-Ghazal area; twenty-five of them died. The trek through malarial and sleepy-sickness country lasted ten weeks, but C.T. kept fit.

He did not feel that was the district for him, however, the need not being great enough; he felt under divine orders to press deep into the Belgian Congo, where there were masses of very evil and destitute people, including pygmies.

5

H.A.M. AND ITS ETCETERAS

"WE have banded ourselves together under the name of *Christ's Etceteras* to make a definite attempt to render the evangelization of the world an accomplished fact. We are merely Christ's nobodies, otherwise Christ's etceteras . . . The funds for this work shall be sought from God only . . . No collection for Etcetera work shall be taken up at any meeting held, or recognized, by this Brotherhood."

So spoke C. T. Studd when he had returned to England from the Sudan full of plans for the New Crusade and had gathered together a group of Christian leaders, who whole-heartedly supported the idea, to be with him in making the necessary decisions.

The Heart of Africa Mission was then formed and the work continues in Central Africa to this day, under the initials H.A.M., though it is now part of the Worldwide Evangelization Crusade,[1] which stemmed out of it, and which will be

[1] Offices now at Bulstrode, Gerrards Cross, Bucks.

described later. The early copies of the H.A.M. magazine were edited by Scilla Studd and printed in the shape of a heart. Bound volumes are to be seen in the Library at the Mission H.Q.

C.T. laid down very definite principles for those taking part in the New Crusade. He stated that Christ's Etceteras were a Christian union mission, and did not belong to any one church; in fact they formed a worldwide missionary crusade. They were to search and find out what parts of the world had not heard the Gospel story, and then "by faith in Christ, by prayer to God, by obedience to the Holy Ghost, by courage, determination, and supreme sacrifice, to accomplish their evangelization". And it must all be done as a matter of great urgency.

So it is obvious that there was no place in the ranks of the Etceteras for anyone who was half-hearted, or who suffered from divided loyalties. The Etcetera Evangelist had to be a man of God, and a servant of God who knew no other master. He must have no doubts about the supplying of his needs for living, knowing that God was able to supply all of them.

The Etcetera man was to carry his "cheque-book"—by which was meant his Bible—with him always. He was to have no fear of the "cheques" being returned to him as duds.

The Etcetera missionary had in God a multi-millionaire to back him up, the wealthiest known to the world. God urged him to draw on the Heavenly Bank, and assured him that the supply would never fail.

The Etceteras would a thousand times rather die trusting only in God than live trusting in men.

Summing up his word-picture of the Etceteras, C.T. said, "We will have the holiness of God, not the sickly stuff of talk and dainty words and pretty thoughts. We will have a masculine holiness, one of daring faith and works for Jesus Christ."

And on the eve of the day on which he set sail for Africa he spoke words which were to become the motto of the New Crusade, "If Jesus Christ be God and died for me, then no sacrifice can be too great for me to make for Him."

As the years passed, missionaries in all parts of the world breathed that motto when faith fell short temporarily, or when the outlook was very grim, and were glad of its tonic effects.

Now all armies—and the Etceteras were most certainly members of a great army, the Christian one—must have a power-station, a headquarters, from which to draw their supplies, and to which to look for leadership, and organization.

All supplies for every kind of need for H.A.M. missionaries were drawn from a sizeable house in a road not far from the famous Crystal Palace, which stood on a hill in South London from which could be seen, right across the city, the hills of Hampstead to the north.

It was about the time that H.A.M. was started that C.T. felt God wanted him to have this house, No. 17 Highland Road, West Norwood, for a H.Q., and the necessary finance was soon obtained. Visits to auctions produced the needed furniture and fittings at an amazingly low cost.

The time came when there was urgent need for expansion. The First World War was on, and Charlie did not feel that he should take any more money responsibility, so when the TO BE LET board went up next door, he did not make enquiries. The house became a Cats' and Dogs' Home, run by an eccentric old lady who did not look after the animals well.

C.T. criticized himself over this loss of the house. "I hadn't the faith to trust God for another £100 a year—I who am always talking about God supplying all our need!"

It was not long, however, before the TO LET notice went up again, and after some hitches, No. 19 became part of the H.Q. And up to the time of C.T.'s death, over £146,000 was sent to Highland Road for the work of the missionaries—a sum of money nearly six times as much as the amount

Studd gave away to Gospel activities when he received the major part of his legacy from his father.

Now there is one most important thing which has not been mentioned yet—a H.Q. must have someone in charge of it. In the case of H.A.M., it was Scilla Studd who took on the work, right from the start. Despite the drawback of not having at all good health, she not only supervised the office work all down the years, but travelled widely, speaking about what the Mission was doing, and calling for men and women to enter God's service in the areas of the world where the natives did not know anything about Him.

So although C.T. had hoped that it was in God's plan for his wife to come out with him to work in the heart of Darkest Africa, he had to acknowledge it was not so. God had a different but just as important a task for her at home. She did, however, spend about a fortnight with him on an African mission station a little while before he died.

Scilla's mission work was, of course, coupled with the care and training of her children, who stood by and stood up for their mother through the years of separation from her beloved husband and their beloved father.

Scilla's character could be summed up in many ways, and from many angles, but here is a quote from one of her favourite addresses, which was headed, *Five packed minutes on a Crazy Mission*:

"Just listen to this extract from a letter from a friend: 'We read your magazine with interest. You are, humanly speaking, one of the craziest missionary societies that ever existed; but if sanity means modernism and no souls saved, may God grant you may never be sane!' And so say all of us!"

That sums it up: "And so say all of us!"

And now, having spent a short while looking into the former H.A.M. headquarters, it is time to return to the period in 1913 when the Etcetera pioneers—C. T. Studd, who was then 52, and Alfred Buxton, not yet 21 and "not over strong" (son of an old Cambridge friend of the famous cricketer), set out on H.A.M.'s first crusade—to trek through Kenya and Uganda to the Congo side of Lake Albert, and there to start a work which was to change vast areas of evil-infested Congo jungle and swamp and scorched earth.

6

BAPTISMS AT "BUCKINGHAM PALACE"

"THE Belgians won't let you in because you're British." That was what Charles Studd and Alfred Buxton were told when, in British East Africa, they mentioned their plan to get into the Belgian Congo. C.T. replied: "That remains to be seen!" and added that he would prove he could enter the Congo. And how right he turned out to be.

While still in East Africa, and on the way to Lake Albert, Alfred had a severe attack of fever which kept him in bed for a week; but when he was well enough, they pressed on, mostly using their bicycles, to Masindi. There a fire in their camp put paid to one of their tents, and a man-eating lion caused them real trouble.

On top of all this, Alfred had a cable from Britain telling him that he was completely unfit for the job, and ordering him to give up the trek, and come home. But he decided that, as an Etcetera, he had been called by God to do this missionary work and must obey Him, and not his relations. It is a fact that in the next two years he didn't have even an hour's fever.

It took them three days to reach the British side of Lake Albert. Having crossed the water they set foot on the soil of the Belgian Congo, which they called their promised land. They were well received by the local official and given permission to stay, with their cycles.

"I'm sorry, Alfred," C.T. said to his companion, smiling, "that those people who said we'd never get in aren't here to see us now! It would do 'em good!"

That night, they camped only a few yards from the water's edge. They had porridge for supper—and a plague of mosquitoes and lake flies, and were not a little scared by the grunting or barking, they were not sure which, of crocodiles, much too close to them for comfort. A good camp fire kept them away, however.

On they went towards Kilo next morning. They found it difficult to get native carriers, but a few agreed to come with them. Their reason was, to the surprise of the missionaries, that they would be with white men.

Unfortunately, very soon the two men became separated from their porters, and had their first taste of the tough trekking problems they would have to face. Choosing the wrong track they spent three hours going up and down very steep hills, often pushing their cycles. They had no food and no money, and only a left-over-from-school-days knowledge of French, and no knowledge at all of the local lingo.

Tired out and very hungry, they were glad to see a native carrying a basket with maize and sweet potatoes in it. They got him to let them have a small supply but were then faced with the problem of paying for the stuff.

C.T. had a brain-wave. "Why do breeches have so many buttons?" he asked himself, and answered "So that some could be cut off and used for money in the wilds of Africa, of course!"

At the next village they found a man who could cook, and although their kit was very poor at present-day standards (no saucepan, no frying-pan), half an hour afterwards they ate with real relish, even though the food had been cooked by putting it actually into the fire.

They found Kilo to be a mining centre. They had to stay there for three months because of transport snags, but were thrilled at receiving their first post. The news came that Dorothy Studd, who had married the Rev. Gilbert A. Barclay, had had a daughter, Ann.

"My first grandchild!" cried C.T., and did a hop, skip and jump. "I do thank God for His goodness."

On to Arebi, and then to Dungu, where they had planned to begin their Gospel work. There they met Count Ferdinand de Grunne, a Roman Catholic official who became a most helpful and truly faithful friend. "No trouble was too much, no kindness too great for him to do for us," C.T. said of him.

The Count smoothed the way for the missionaries to get good concessions of land for building mission-stations in a number of places, including their first "stop", which had to be Niangara instead of Dungu.

In the very heart of Africa, Niangara was an area of luxurious vegetation, grassland and little villages with grass-thatched huts, set in the middle of plantations of palms or bananas.

It was October 16, 1913, when Charles and Alfred, at the end of their first long and arduous trek, camped in the place where they were to build their first mission-station, and to call it "Buckingham Palace".

Niangara's "Buckingham Palace" was built in a few weeks for about £6. It was 75 feet in length, 35 feet in width, and there was also a round shed-like building for native palavers.

Putting it in just those few words makes it all sound very simple, but never make the mistake of thinking that because you are serving in a faith mission everything goes right first time. Though it generally comes right in the end.

It was like that at Niangara, set in one of the most thickly-populated districts of the Congo, many of the natives being pygmies, who were extremely hard to contact in the depths of the forests.

Charles and Alfred set out to look for a suitable site but found considerable difficulties and had to go much farther than they had expected. About to give up the search, they spotted a lovely grove of palm trees.

"This is it!" cried C.T. "We'll come back tomorrow and start to clear the site."

As soon as they got to work, the local village headman came and told them they could not have the land. The missionaries showed how disappointed they were, so the man said he knew of a better site on higher ground. C.T. thanked him, and the headman took them to see it.

C.T.'s eyes shone when he saw it. "This is the place, Alfred!" he said to his companion. "There is a spring, good soil, and a splendid lot of palm trees. We'll come back tomorrow and start to clear the ground."

Which they did. Until a band of natives arrived on the scene and showed quite definitely that the "visitors" were not welcome or wanted, and that they could not start building there.

Charles and Alfred held a "council of war" and decided to go to Nala, five days' trek to the south, which they had heard was a good centre. Arrived there, C.T. felt strongly drawn to the place and applied at once for land for building. Returning to Niangara, only a few days had passed before the pioneer was told he could build mission-stations in both places, the Count having intervened on his behalf.

Having arranged for the building to start in Niangara, the two men set off to explore deeper into the forests and get to Medje and Nepolo. On the way they found tribes, who had been at war only a few months before, now more peaceful and quite prepared to be friendly. In fact in some villages, the "locals" became a bit of a problem. Probably the cycles were a greater attraction than the missionaries themselves.

"Day after day they ran along in front and behind our cycles, shouting, laughing and singing their chants; you never heard such a din, nor so much enthusiasm!" was C.T.'s description. It was like an excited crowd surging round the pavilion after a test match.

They would struggle to get the chance to carry the bikes across streams, rivers and dilapidated bridges, which looked as though they would collapse at any moment under the weight of the surging people. They pleaded to carry the bikes up and down gullies and ravines. Sometimes the crowd was as large as 500, so the white men had a job to keep pace with them, and had not the breath to laugh and shout and sing with the natives.

Whenever there had to be a pause for rest, the two missionaries took every opportunity to tell the tribespeople something of the story of Jesus and His love.

C.T. summed it all up to Alfred by saying: "Well, here is our 'Eldorado'. Here is a land and a people to whom the Name of Jesus has never been spoken. Shall we leave them like this? We will not! They shall hear the Gospel story, and many will heed the Saviour's call."

But the problem on their minds for some while was the urgent need for helpers, so they were thrilled one day to hear by post that their prayers had been answered and that five were on the way from Britain.

C.T. then decided this was the right time for him to leave Alfred in charge, and travel the 700 miles down the Congo river to its mouth on the Atlantic coast, and there to sail home to tour the country and enlist more recruits.

Alfred returned to the Niangara/Nala district to find that the people there were more keen than before to hear about Jesus and His love. And what a thrill it was for him to perform the first baptismal service to be held in the Niangara mission-station. He baptized twelve believers.

Six months later there was an even greater thrill for Buxton, for he baptized eighteen converts, the first of whom was an ex-cannibal named Sambo. There were other cannibals, murderers, drunkards, thieves, sex-sinners and swearers.

Some of the confessions made before the act of baptism show what a terrific change had come over the men. "My father killed a man and I helped to eat him." "When I was three years old I remember my father killing a man, and because he had killed my brother, I shared in eating the stew." "I have done more sin than there is room for in my chest." "I did witchcraft from the finger-nails of a dead man."

One of the early converts used his experience of cannibalism to save C.T. from certain death. There was serious disorder one day among men from a wild river tribe who were paddling the missionary's canoe down the Aruwimi river. The canoe was rocking from side to side dangerously as the paddlers shouted and yelled at C.T.; but in the nick of time, the convert shouted back, "Get on with your work! Remember, in my time I have eaten better men than you."

All went well after that.

*   *   *

Studd reached England safely, and returned to his beloved African jungle in July 1916. There were eight in the party, one being his daughter Edith on her way to marry Alfred Buxton.

The party had a marvellous welcome at Nala, where there were now over 60 Christians. Old Sambo did a whole day's trek to be present, and C.T. described the procession as like a Lord Mayor's Show.

The item which probably delighted him most was four men carrying on their heads a huge wooden drum on which was perched a small black boy beating away with all his might.

Then followed the Welcome Home service, and C.T. was "much struck with the quietness of the natives at worship; their reverence was in inverse proportion to the comfort of their seats", which were benches made out of three long broomsticks about an inch apart. A different kind of witchcraft!

Then came another "first" for Niangara. The first white wedding in the Heart of Africa. And it took place in "Buckingham Palace". The religious service was followed by a tribal feast, and that by the legal service of twenty minutes, at which the local Belgian officials were present in full dress uniforms with medals and Orders—a delightful compliment to Alfred and Edith, and a tribute to C.T.'s Christian leadership in the district.

7

THE MONKEY THAT DISAPPEARED

"I WAS a great warrior. I used to be sent by the Belgians to take villages and chiefs which they wanted to be subdued. At one time I became very ill and lost all consciousness and died," was what Jabori said about his part before he and eighty more natives were baptized at Nala, among them three chiefs, two of whom had built chapels in their villages.

"My friends had dug my grave, and were putting me into it," Jabori went on, "when I rose up and said I had seen God Himself, who told me that before long the English would come and tell us all about the true God, and the truth. I told this vision to many, who were struck, and because of this, the people used to speak of God by the name 'English'."

C.T., who had now made Nala his H.Q., said of Jabori's amazing confession, "God still works by giving dreams to these people. If *every* conversion in Britain is a miracle, *any* conversion in Africa is a thousand times greater miracle.

"Can you faintly imagine the condition of things when public opinion is on the side of sin, and when such a situation has been there for hundreds of years? The lives of people become lower than the brute beasts."

But natives kept on being changed from vicious and witchcraft-loving heathen; and to gladden C.T.'s heart even more, numbers of them felt the urge to go out preaching, for periods of as long as three months, in the surrounding villages, and on the rivers. Outreach work, it would be called today.

There were about twenty in the first batch of raw but most enthusiastic native evangelists to go out from Nala. They were paid three francs each for the twelve weeks to cover all outgoings, and yet some came back with one franc and some with half that amount, and put the money into the church bank from which it had been taken.

They had to carry all their kit all the time. Usually there were a grass-mat bed, a thin blanket, a food basket carried under the belt, from which hung a jungle knife and an enamel cup. Their only clothing was loin cloths, and they delighted in showing off their homemade straw hats, which they usually wore at a jaunty angle. In very hot weather they were heavily oiled all over so that they glistened in the tropical sunshine.

Of course C.T. still went on trek, but being a white man, he had to have five porters to carry his luggage. He still used his cycle a great deal.

One day he could not get away to see Chief Aboramasi until late afternoon, so the party had to camp overnight. The porters were up very early next day, but C.T. followed a while later on his bike. He came to a wide and flooded stream, and stood there scratching his head and wondering how he was to get across. Then he saw a young fellow on the opposite bank who came at his call, carried the bike across and then returned for the cyclist.

The young fellow heaved C.T. on to his back, walked a few yards into the water, wobbled—and fell forward, pitching the missionary over his head.

"There was nothing for it but to let out a good guffaw," said C.T. of the incident, "and go one's way rejoicing, like the Ethiopian in Acts did after his baptism."

Possibly Charles remembered then the time when he was on a different kind of transport—a mule. Suddenly he saw in front of him a fallen tree forming a narrowing arch across the track. Could he get through without dismounting? He did not have time to decide, for the mule made for the tree, and C.T. became stuck between the arches where they narrowed towards the top. He managed to get himself through, but he injured his left side.

"I felt like a pancake when I got through the arch," he said. "Ribs a bit crushed and very painful even when I was sitting. But thank God for keeping me thin! It just about saved the day for me."

When the missionary caught up with his porters on the way to Chief Aboramasi, there was a second event which had its humorous side. He found the porters were arguing with a man over the buying of a large monkey which he had shot. C.T. butted in and bought the animal, because it was good food for the porters, and because he wanted the skin to mend his banjo.

He never saw the monkey again, however, nor any part of it. It went into the soup, probably.

There was a third snag, of course. When the party got going again, from one of the porter-carried boxes a dark liquid started to run out. Somehow C.T.'s home-made treacle tin had been turned upside-down, and the lid had come loose.

Papers, books, letters, clothes all became very sticky. It took two hours to clear up the mess, so that when the party arrived at Aboramasi's village, it was dark and they were very tired, and ready to bed down for the night.

But the villagers had no such idea in their minds. They wanted a sing-song of hymns in the moonlight, followed by a service.

The next day there was almost continuous worship, and a lantern service in the evening at which Bwana (Chief) not only had to work the lantern but to explain the pictures, too.

C.T. did not speak the local Bangala language well, so after a while he said to one of the native leaders, "Now, it's your innings. They may not have understood my edition, so give them yours."

So the leader began, but his voice was drowned by the chieftain and his people crying out, "Wapi! Wapi!", which meant "Stuff and nonsense!" They said they understood Bwana's every word.

At the close of the service, Aboramasi spoke and gave C.T. a wonderful thrill when he said, "I and my people, and my brother chief and his people, desire to tell you that we believe these things about God and Jesus and ourselves, and we all want to travel the same road as you—the road to heaven."

*   *   *

The time came when Alfred Buxton and his wife and baby daughter Susan (the first white baby born in the Heart of Africa, and who was dedicated in the Nala Church) went to Britain on furlough. The six missionaries now left in the area held on bravely, but it was a time of severe testing, for many converts fell back into their sinful ways.

But while things were going back in that part of Africa, in Britain there was a striking forward move following the end of the First World War. In 1919 Gilbert Barclay, husband of Dorothy (Studd), joined the staff at Highland Road, South London, as Home Overseer. He was a tower of strength to Mrs Scilla Studd.

Barclay at once began to stress the original idea of the New Crusade as an all-the-world mission, and a new title for the work was adopted. It was the Worldwide Evangelization Crusade. Each new area had its own title also, on the lines of the Heart of Africa Mission.

No. 2 Crusade was the Heart of Amazonia Mission, in which Fenton Hall (who lost his life) and Kenneth Grubb and Harold Morris (who were tortured and almost starved to death) were the missionaries.

No. 3 Crusade was to Central Asia, and Jock Purves and Rex Bavington got beyond the northern frontiers of India, crossing into Little Tibet by a 16,000-ft. high pass in the Himalayas.

Crusade No. 4 was to Arabia and No. 5 to West Africa. Both failed at the first attempt, but later the Heart of Arabia Mission (Jack Wilson) was set up to tell the Gospel story to the Bedouins.

No. 6 Crusade (Pat Symes) was to the people of Colombia, in South America.

As the years passed by, more and more men and women joined the W.E.C. and went abroad to take their part in the worldwide crusade.

* * *

But to return to Africa, new staff came out to C.T. in 1920, and when Alfred Buxton returned a year later, he took over the leadership at Nala, so C.T. set out to grasp the opportunities which he had seen to be everywhere in the Ituri Province when he had spent a short while in the forest area some years before.

There he was to see the most amazing success of his career, with thousands giving up their heathen customs and using their lives to spread the Gospel.

8

CROWDS THRONG CRICKET-PITCH
CHURCH

"I'M going to get them to build a church here,"
said C. T. Studd to his white companion when
on a visit from the village of Ibambi to Imbai,
five hours' trek through the forest, "and I'm going
to plan it to be a cricket-pitch length each way!
We'll call it the Cricket-Pitch Church, and it will
have to hold at least 1,250 people."

C.T. found Imbai a most thrilling project, for
the natives were very eager to hear the Gospel.
Before the church was built—in record time—the
Congolese came from all points of the compass to
Imbai, singing all the way. Once 1,500 of them
squatted on the ground, packed as tight as fish in a
tin. They sat in the tropical sun for two hours,
were made to take an hour's rest, and then came
back for another two hours of worship.

The building of the church was an all-out job,
and when the time came for the roof to be
"thatched", the grass had to be got and carried
quite a distance. A missionary suggested that the

workers should go back to their villages, and return in a few days to finish. The natives did not like that idea at all. "Do you think we're going home with the House of God unfinished?"

They stayed on till the job was done—*and* a little hut built for the missionary.

The work progressed in Imbai, once known as the hunting ground of the fiercest leopards. It became a fine mission-station, with schools, sheds for do-it-yourself training, new homes for the missionaries, new church, streets of huts for the natives, and good areas for growing food.

The chieftain, usually an on-the-quiet-side Christian, gave the Belgian officials a real surprise one day. Ordered to come and see them, Imbai listened quietly while the chosen official spoke.

"You have our permission, Chief Imbai, to charge the Mission a yearly rent of about 600 francs for the use of your land," the official said, and the sum he quoted was a small fortune to a chieftain in those days.

Imbai did not hesitate. "I will not do any such thing!"

The statement was repeated, but Imbai gave the same answer, and added: "I have given the land to God, and so I could not think of making anything out of it!"

Bwana Studd often visited Imbai. The village

drummers would pass on the news of his coming, and off men, women and children would go for the main service to be held about mid-day, usually in the open-air under the palm trees, because the church could not hold the crowd of 2,000.

They certainly believed in getting plenty of Gospel food! On Sunday, especially. First there would be an hour of hymn-singing. C.T. had about 100 hymns, written by himself in the local lingo, which he accompanied on his banjo. Many of the hymns had good actions to go with them, and there were plenty of "Hallelujahs!"

There followed as much as forty minutes of fervent thrilling prayers spoken by the natives, and every one ending with "*ku jina ya Yesu*", which means "in the Name of Jesus". This would be repeated in every case by the whole congregation.

Reading the Scriptures (on which the 90 to 120 minutes' sermon would be based), and saying the Commandments together, would come next; and in the address (which in later years he would give seated) C.T. always made a point of picturing the people in the Bible stories in African fashion. And, of course, "bread" became "bananas", "camels" became "elephants", and chalk took the place of snow, which was unknown to his hearers.

And sometimes, if the families had brought their

75

sleeping mats and their food with them, the services would go on through Monday and even Tuesday.

Chief Adzangwe was another of C.T.'s best friends. As many as 500 used to come to his village for worship.

After a while, wonderful things happened at Adzangwe's village, under the leadership of their chieftain, who had been one of the worst cannibals, and a ringleader in all kinds of evil actions and customs. Earlier on, he had claimed to have been converted, but it had not been a real change. Now he was altogether different. He became a 100 per cent evangelist himself and did his best to get the other chiefs around to believe in Jesus. He sent out natives to take the Gospel to distant tribes.

What splendid witnesses many of the converts were! Take, for example, a man, beaten under orders of his chieftain for telling about Jesus, who did not protest over this treatment, but, the beating over, held out his hand to the chieftain saying, "Thank you for giving me the honour of having a beating for Jesus."

He was given another beating for replying like that. After it, this time he stayed on his knees and prayed aloud for the chief. When he was jailed, very soon some of his fellow-believers went to the chief, and said, "May we have the honour of being put in prison for Jesus along with our brother believer?"

It is not known what the chief said to that.

But perhaps Zamu was the most amazing convert in Adzangwe's village. He got the call to become a missionary and trekked some 200 miles from his home base, contacting the wildest of all tribes. This is how it all came about.

Zamu was "an insignificant little man" who suffered terribly from an ulcer on one leg which would not heal, and which made it necessary for him to walk on the toes of one foot. He was already in trouble with the officials and with other tribes because of his passion for evangelism in the nearby villages.

When, however, he heard about tribes in the distant south who had been enemies of his tribe for generations, and had killed and put into slavery his own people, he felt chosen by God to go to them, and he was sure his work would be successful.

"But won't it be death for me," he said to himself, "if I go to such wild people without any protection from the white men?"

Then he saw a vision of Christ on the Cross, put there by His enemies, nailed there for the sins of the whole world, including the vicious tribes-people he was thinking about.

77

He told the woman missionary who was at Adzangwe's village at that time that he felt he must go far away to the tribes beyond the present mission area.

Realizing the very great danger he would be in, and the trouble with his leg, the missionary put a number of questions to him to test his decision. But to every one he replied, "God is, White Lady," even including the one about taking his wife with him. "She will accompany me. God is, White Lady."

Off they set, and the first part of the trek took them to Ibambi. They called on C.T., and had a good talk.

"Go on from day to day as God gives you strength, Zamu," was Bwana's advice. "God will be with you, and He will keep you. Don't be afraid. Be bold and preach the Gospel—and if you are true, God will make you a great company one day."

The first stage was eighty miles through the forest, crossing the Ituri river; and then, making south to the Babari tribe, he added another 100 miles to his distance from home.

On to the Balumbi tribe, who received him in a friendly way, though they could not understand a black man who didn't do any of the awful things they did. They called him "The Stray Man".

Everything was all right until he started pointing out how wicked they were, and pleaded with them to give up their evil customs. Then they turned on him and his wife, who very nearly starved.

But God had the situation in hand. The brother of the local chief, who had agreed with what Zamu was saying, invited him and his wife to his garden, and told them to eat all they needed and take some for the future.

Despite this kindness, the uninteresting food, which did not include salt or palm fat, was getting them down. Finally, Zamu made a special prayer about it.

"O Lord, You have kept Your messengers from starvation, but we long for a little salt. Send us this, dear Lord, as a token that You are with us."

The answer to this prayer was as unexpected as it was amazing. At that very moment, reinforcements from his home church were on the way to Zamu and his wife, and, two weeks later, the couple saw a party of (they thought) strangers coming down the village street. Recognizing them, they ran into each others' arms—and the newcomers handed over a large packet of salt.

Some years later there were ten evangelists working among the Balumbis. Zamu's venture of faith stirred fifty native pioneers and their wives from Adzangwe's church to penetrate to six new tribes.

So C.T. in his later years saw a native church filled with the Holy Spirit's power, and with service to God the keynote of their lives. "Oh, it is good to be in a stiff fight for Jesus!" he wrote home. "The work is reaching a sure foundation, and we'll soon be bounding forward!"

C.T. visited Adzangwe's village when the chief was dying. The old man refused to stay in his sick bed, and was lifted in a chair and carried to the missionary's house. Bwana moved out slowly to meet the chief, and missionaries brought a chair for C.T. to sit on and some cushions.

But C.T., who was then as weak as Adzangwe, took the cushions from his chair and placed them round the body of the one-time cannibal chief so that he should sit as comfortably as possible.

That was the last time they met on earth.

9

BWANA'S "ADOPTED FAMILY"

IT was about the same time that those working under the new mission title of The Worldwide Evangelization Crusade went into Amazonia on Crusade No. 2, that C. T. Studd decided to make his permanent H.Q. at the village of Ibambi.

One item of evidence showing the importance of the place as a big population centre was that, for miles leading up to it, the forest had been cleared to the depth of five cricket-pitches on either side of the track.

There were many lovely palm trees with neat bamboo huts built under their shade. The roofs were of leaves, as were the doors. The natives had their hair carefully plaited in many weird "styles", which looked even queerer because they were based on very long heads, on which often sat crazy straw hats.

When C.T., now most often called Bwana, came to Ibambi, his aquiline nose was even more pronounced in a face with sunken cheeks, partly due to the loss of most of his teeth. His figure was gaunt and his beard thick. He looked what he was, a fervent prophet, but his stern look and flashing eyes were relieved by his sense of humour, and cheerful laughter. His jokes, however, were a brand of his very own.

Thousands were crying out to be taught about God and His love, and many hundreds flocked to Ibambi to be baptized.

"We were besieged by people coming for baptism," wrote C.T. to the home folks. "Almost every day one could hear the hymns of people coming from various directions to confess Jesus as their Saviour."

New out-stations were opened up in at least six areas, and to these, too, the natives flocked. This was indeed the spiritual Eldorado of which C.T. had spoken earlier.

But the work was very tiring, and Bwana was pressed from Britain, and by his companions in Africa, to go on furlough. Time and again he refused to listen to this reasoning.

"God told me to go out to Africa when every voice was raised against me," was his reply, "and only God can tell me when to go home."

C.T.'s health had been a matter of considerable worry to his fellow missionaries for a long time, and a while later one of them tried to approach the problem of getting him to go on furlough from another, and very personal angle.

"You really ought to go home and get your teeth properly seen to," he said. "For some while you've had to live mostly on slops, and this must have reduced your strength very greatly."

But the answer was still in the negative.

"Not even my teeth trouble—and the suffering has been very small really in comparison with the Saviour's, hasn't it?—will make me change my mind. And if God wants me to have some new teeth," and his smile showed his lack of the old ones, "He can just as easily send me some here."

Some months later, Pauline (Studd) and her husband, Norman Grubb, on their way back to Britain, were travelling by native canoe down the Aruwimi to its junction with the Congo river.

Early one morning during their fortnight's journey they saw another canoe coming towards them up-river, and there was a white man in it! As the boats came within hailing distance, the Grubbs called out a greeting in English, and a reply came back in the same language.

"Let's pull into the bank and have breakfast together," was suggested.

On landing the three Britishers introduced themselves, the newcomer being a Mr. Buck. They went a short way into the forest for shade, had a meal, and then prayed together. At parting Mr. Buck took hold of Mrs. Grubb's arm and drew her aside.

"As you are a daughter of Mr. Studd," he said, "I'd like to tell you a secret. God has sent me to the Heart of Africa not only to preach the Gospel, but also to provide Mr. Studd with a set of teeth. I've brought with me all that is necessary for making and fitting them."

Mrs. Grubb's eyes lit up at this amazing news, and after they had talked a little longer, she and her husband set off down-stream, while the new-comer went on his way to Ibambi.

Arrived there, he introduced himself to C.T. and said, "The first thing that God sent me to the Congo to do was your teeth." And it was not long before the remaining over-worked molars were out, and plans made for the new teeth.

"How wonderful God is, sending a dentist to the Heart of Africa to look after the teeth of His child who couldn't return home! But remember I said," he reminded those around him, "that God could easily send me some new teeth out here, if He wanted me to have them!"

And how had Dentist Buck come to be on the Aruwimi river that day he met the Grubbs? Months before he had written to the London H.Q. and offered himself for service with the

Heart of Africa Mission, but as he was ten years over age, his offer had been rejected.

Nothing daunted, he sold his practice, and obtained a passage to the mouth of the Congo river. When he got there, he set up a surgery for officials and traders, and soon had the necessary money to travel the 700-plus miles up-river into the Ituri district.

Was his a chance meeting with Mr. and Mrs. Grubb? They did not think so, and neither did the dentist.

It is easy to realize the sensation that the appearance of Bwana with his new white teeth caused when he faced his first congregation (of 1,000) wearing them. But he had by no means got used to what he called "the adopted family" in his mouth, and he took them out while someone else was praying.

The praying over, imagine the amazement on the black faces when they saw the teeth had gone. "Who has pulled out Bwana's new teeth while we've all been praying?" they asked themselves.

C.T. had a joke on his "boys" one day. He put in the lower plate without pressing it into position, and when they came in, he sat on a stool, reached for a pair of pliers and yanked out the eight teeth with one pull. The faces of the "boys" would have made a classic snapshot.

C.T. never really got used to the new teeth, and, although he did manage to eat more solid food, his health continued to decline. His teeth were often to be seen on his writing table, in use as a pen and pencil stand.

C.T.'s home in Ibambi was a circular hut with bamboo walls, dried mud floor and grass roof. A chieftain gave him his bed, which had no springs. Goat hide straps were attached to the wooden frame, and C.T. lay on a number of well-worn blankets, and had some on top of him. His head rested on canvas pillows.

At one side of his bed was a table, the top of which was rather like a schoolboy's. It was covered with all sorts of things, from scissors and knives to pens and pencils, small carpentry tools and the like. A number of different editions of the Bible were on a bookshelf opposite, his favourite being the Revised Version.

Bwana's home was a "bed-sit", his only warmth (needed when the temperature dropped suddenly) coming from a log fire built up on the floor near the foot of his bed. On cold nights his "boy", called One Leg because he had a stiff limb, lay close to the fire, waking like clockwork each morning at 3 a.m. to make his beloved master a cup of tea.

Then One Leg would return to his position by

the fire, and go to sleep again, while C.T. would read his Bible.

This was his only sermon-preparation time, and he never needed more for that day's work.

He was a stickler for strict attention to detail in material things, even the minor ones. This was because he knew very well how bad an influence laziness had on the natives.

A close friend visiting the Bwana saw him set a small boy the job of finding a button the lad had lost; not because the object was valuable, which it was not, but so as to teach carefulness. And he kept the boy on the search for a whole day!

Mail from Europe came once a fortnight on Saturdays. C.T. would spend most of the day replying to his correspondents; then a native would be called. Given a spear and a lantern, he would set off through the night forest to hand over the mail to an official runner at the end of a twelve-hour trek.

The time came when Bwana, much against his will, realized that he could no longer walk or cycle on his Gospel tours. He had to be carried in a mandala, sitting on a canvas seat, with native mats above him for protection from wind and rain.

Ten volunteers were his carriers using long

bamboo poles, one each side of the "sedan chair", with two men at the front and two at the back. The carriers had fine voices, and the forest tracks would resound with their singing.

10

ONE OF GOD'S "MYSTERIOUS WAYS"

"WE are gloriously discontented with the condition of the Native Church. It is all very well to sing hymns and go to worship, but what we *must* see are the 'fruits of the Spirit', and a really changed life and heart, a hatred of sin, and a passion for righteousness."

The "gloriously discontented" was a typically C. T. Studd way of describing a situation, but he and his fellow missionaries at Ibambi were deeply concerned because, after some years of remarkable advance, with thousands in and around Ibambi baptized, tragic signs of a decline in worship and witness were becoming all too obvious.

Apart from a return to being lazy and forgetful (which were chief characteristics of the Congolese) bringing with them lack of interest in prayer, worship, Scripture study and the like, there was a return to idolatry, witchcraft and sorcery, and even baptized believers were taking part in the ghastly practices of the tribal secret societies.

The general idea among so many of those who

had said they believed in the Gospel, and so had been baptized, was that, having done this, they were all right for this world and for the next. So it didn't matter how much they lied, deceived, stole, sinned sexually, or went back to ancient tribal customs which they now felt had served them well in their day.

In some places there was even open hostility by one-time believers. As it had been at Nala, so in Ibambi it became a time of anxiety and sorrow.

This was the biggest non-personal problem C.T. ever had to face. He was certain that the only cure for the backsliding was a baptism of the Holy Spirit, such as is described in Acts 2 as happening at Pentecost.

This could not be "ordered"; it could only come when God sent it; and it could only come on people who were ready to receive it, knowing all it meant in sacrifice and service, and who were willing to give themselves completely to Him.

The burden was certainly not lightened by differences among the missionaries because of C.T.'s refusal to move an inch from his standards of simple faith, simple living and complete sacrifice of personal desires and personal comfort. Even some of the London H.Q. committee were out of step with the H.A.M. founder, but he wouldn't even discuss any changes in belief or organization.

And so the battle on two fronts went on . . . until C.T. came to Prayers one unforgettable night in Ibambi. Eight missionaries were gathered around him. Obviously he had the major problem very much in mind as he suggested they read together from his beloved Hebrews the chapter (11) about the Heroes of Faith. And what a fabulous list it is!

"What noble and utter sacrifices they made! How God honoured and blessed them, each in their different ways—and made them a blessing for others in their lifetime—yes and now here as we read and think and pray together tonight.

"What was the Spirit which caused these very human people so to triumph and die? The Holy Spirit of God . . . This is *our* need tonight. Will God give to us as He gave to them? Yes! Yes! Yes! What are the conditions? God gives *all* to those who give Him *their* all."

The missionaries began to talk over with C.T. what he had said (of which the above is but a tiny extract) and someone used the illustration of the sacrifice that a soldier makes when he goes "over the top"—for it was mostly trench warfare in those days.

How could this man's spirit best be described? An ex-soldier-missionary replied, "Well, the way the sergeant-major would describe it is that

Tommy doesn't care a d— what happens to him so long as he does his duty by his King, his country, his regiment—and himself."

Some may think it not a little strange that such a sentence should be the sparking-off point for a complete change in the situation, but it was. It was one of those "mysterious ways" in which the hymn tells us God moves to perform His wonders.

C.T. got up, raised his arm and cried out, "That's what we need in Ibambi, and that's what *I* want! So long as Jesus is glorified, I won't care *what* happens to me!"

One by one the other missionaries made the same promise to God, and as they did so, their eyes lit up with a new vision and a new resolve to fight the good fight with even more God-given might than ever before.

The blessing that followed the prayer session that night spread far and wide—to the remotest mission-stations, and to native churches, old and new. What stories could be told of those days! Though they were brought about by changes in individuals rather than by mass conversions.

It would probably be true to say that it was a labour of love which used up most of C.T.'s rapidly-declining strength in the later years. The natives in his area *must* have some parts of the

Bible preserved in their own words. Kingwana was the Iruti Province language; he must translate as much as he could of the New Testament into it.

He worked an 18-hour day, starting at 2 a.m. for a 4-hour spell. One of his comrades, Jack Harrison, typed as the old man translated. At last C.T. finished the New Testament; then he did Psalms, and followed this with extracts from Proverbs. But the strain led to heart attacks, and he had to resort to taking morphine, under medical advice, in order to be able to work and preach.

Some forty missionaries were at work in the Ituri Province as C.T.'s health got worse. They were like his own children to him, their loving care being a great joy, as was a surprise visit of his wife Scilla to Ibambi.

A crowd of 2,000 gathered to greet her. Scilla spoke to them then, and a number of other times during her visit, using an interpreter. The natives fell in love with Mama Bwana, and wanted to hear more about how, in Britain, she was seeking to find more and more men and women to come and tell them about this Jesus. Some of them talked among themselves about how much it must have cost Bwana to be separated from such a lovely wife for so long.

By that time some motor roads had been built in the Ituri area, and the Ibambi station had a car, which was the only means of transport C.T. could use now.

When parting time came, Scilla was obviously under great strain. She walked down the path to the car, eyes straight in front, not seeing the missionaries waiting to say goodbye. With set face, she stepped into the car, and was driven off, not looking back.

That was the last time the Studds saw each other on earth, for Scilla died the year after her Ibambi visit. Charles died two years later.

There were more than 1,500 natives at his funeral, including four chiefs, Kotinaye, Owesi, Abaya and Simba (the last being a name which became world-known in the terrible days following Congo Independence).

*　　*　　*

It was John Bunyan who said: "Sink or swim, come heaven or hell, Lord Jesus . . . I will venture for Thy name." That is exactly what C. T. Studd had spent most of his life doing, and now he had gone to his reward.

How best can the meaning and purpose of his

life be summed up? Perhaps four lines of verse that he often quoted could do it:

> "Some want to live within the sound
> Of church or chapel bell:
> I want to run a rescue shop
> Within a yard of hell."

That is in the true C. T. Studd tradition. And there is another line—this time again from Bwana's beloved Hebrews 11—which fits into the picture perfectly.

It is "He being dead yet speaketh". The story of the harvest of converts and of the amazing outreach of the Worldwide Evangelization Crusade down the years since their beloved Founder's death, gives almost unbelievable but positive proof that the work and witness and personal sacrifice of such men of faith as C. T. Studd live for ever.